Jewel

PEADAR O'DONOGHUE

salmonpoetry

Published in 2012 by
Salmon Poetry
Cliffs of Moher, County Clare, Ireland
Website: www.salmonpoetry.com
Email: info@salmonpoetry.com

ISBN 978-1-908836-02-1

COVER PHOTOGRAPHY: *Peadar O'Donoghue*
COVER DESIGN: *Siobhán Hutson*

Salmon Poetry receives financial support from The Arts Council

For all my family

Acknowledgements

Acknowledgements are due to the editors of the following, in which some of the poems in this collection first appeared:

The SHOp, Revival, Poetry Ireland Review, and online at Bare Hands Poetry and The First Cut.

Thanks to all my family. A huge thanks to Collette for her love, support and understanding through all the years. To Paddy, Mum, Dad (RIP), Mena, Charlie and Angela, and to Mollie for being there when the rest of the world is in bed.

More thanks to John and Hilary Wakeman for their unfailing inspiration, encouragement and kindness. To Ian Duhig for his poetry and taking the time and care to read this book, also Richard W. Halperin. To Karen O'Shea and Rachel Fox for proofreading (blame them if you see any mistakes!) and to every blogger and Facebook pal.

Finally for just about saving my life I'm indebted to the incredible Jessie Lendennie and Siobhán Hutson of Salmon Poetry. Every dog should have its day and they against all the odds have given me mine.

Contents

'Every dog has its day'... I was never a diamond,
not even a rough one, I can't polish pearls of wisdom,
but this is my Jewel.

Jewel

Along Capel Street I stagger into Slattery's
and stagger out again to be sure I have my wits.
What the hell have they done?
Is nothing sacred?
Is anything safe from their blandiose renaissance?
A curse on them whoever they are.
I barrel on to the Quays singing or talking to myself,
corpulent with drink and struggling
to re-inflate between bursts of song.
Filled with stupid elation
and fuelled on pints of stout,
I gaze wide-eyed and blowing
at the new-found beauty of herself,
Anna Liffey.
Spanned by an arch the whiter shade of pale,
her waters are expressive, fecund, and inviting.
With undulating, warm, open arms of green
she calls to me in clamshells of desire.
Wanting to be smothered within
and bursting for a leak,
I express myself,
let fly the floodgates,
a stream of pee to the pea green below,
relief and satisfaction in equal measure.
They'll never take the piss out of Dublin.

Pictures and Postcards

Mountains to mist, Beckett to boxer to blonde –
platinum of course, looking me straight in the eye
over the slope of her shoulder.
She says nothing, and a million things.
Not one can I catch as, like the accusations, I fly.
I'm back on the midnight bus as it pulls out and pulls in
passengers from the random roundabouts of my youth,
girlfriends dressed to kill and dying from the cold.
Yards and years away are barges passing,
coal powered, just like the square panes of light from the
Arndale block that lure people like moths.
The bigger picture hints of a hunt, of war, of winter,
brothers in arms, their quarry sought, their silence confident,
reflective, pleased with themselves, and whatever they have done.
I remember their faces peering in from the streets to the dreamy cafés
'Stay a while', they seem to say. 'Drink your coffee,
compile this list for lesser days.'

At my wake

Inconspicuous in my absence,
eyes thumbed shut,
best-suited arms stiff by my side,
unable to reach the tasty snacks or
pour a pint down the parched gullet.
Deaf ears cannot hear how much they miss me,
on the rigor mortis scale - I'm ten.
Even when young they said
I was 'Dead-but-for-the-washing.'
Do I remember the last supper? Butter on toast
on Sunday, before the mourning on Monday,
the craic here now on Tuesday
I'll be ashes by Wednesday.
Time's still winding clocks and watches like clockwork,
there will be clean shirts at Easter,
roasting hot days in summer with
tar bubbles bursting for joy.
If you take a walk as far as the bridge,
or the canal, buy me a red lemonade
in a black glass in Gleeson's -
at least I was never the poor craythur with a choc ice,
trying to keep his teeth in.

Troglodytes, Troglodytes

I pity the poor wren this Stephen's Day,
tortured, tormented, traitor.
Persecuted for his inadvertent roll upon the drums,
raising the alarm, betraying the cause
in his hungry search for crumbs.

Now we are so sure of our sense of self, without sensibility,
that here in our silk Celtic tiger-striped pyjamas
amongst all the wrappings, discarded toys and turkey bones,
we pluck and cluck, plum-puddin'-blind and indifferent
to his plight; our own; or anybody else's.

The kiss of death

I was the King of Spain and she was the Queen.
We fought with pillows, feathers and hammers,
through the fever of ourselves.
White canaries sang on the windowsill,
galleons rose on tall black seas as
day and night in battle we fell.
The heat of her made me sweat,
hot hands and thighs all over me,
painted nails clutching at my heart.
She was beautiful, too beautiful, her
soft words were spoken, barely whispered
sweet nothings, in breathy deathly lust.
She wanted me so bad, if I but closed my eyes
and kissed her lips, I was gone.

Johannes Greenberg's Nude with Masks (1931)

Even as I waited for the light in her eyes,
my stare was drawn, weak to
the bronze of her flesh –
another mask.
I had seen her nude before, but never naked,
and as she pulled away,
I took my only chance,
traded truth for lies,
and cloths for heaven.

Us

Are they swifts or swallows, I can never tell
and did either of them ever make a summer anyway?
Hard to believe now, in the detritus
and deus ex machina of our lives,
as we look with cool autumnal stare,
that once vital, we loved, and bobbed and weaved,
upon the wing, dewy-eyed and without a care.

After the Deluge

Not quite darkness, not quite wilderness,
not quite wandering.
More surely walking, wandering,
balanced on
the converging parallels of talking and listening,
grabbing at tricoloured stars
to steady me
as they pass around words
like theological iodine tablets
for the fallout from the nuclear bomb,
branded as fireworks.
We are the vicarious walking wounded,
countless others, lives, families, selves,
blown to pieces,
if not kingdom-come.
Would their,
if only their
kingdom would come.
For how else,
where else,
do we go from here?

Starfish on the Beach

I was looking for hares, foxes, rabbits
on the hillside,
I was reaching for things out of reach,
for unlimited words to make sense of me,
trying not to grow old too quick,
running away by standing still.

This was wintertime,
there was no escaping that,
look at the sea, the skies,
the dead looks of trees
bereft of, mournful for, their leaves
blown to the four winds and corners of
the earth.

Wave after wave, tide after tide,
singing us the song of winter,
Christmas come and gone,
a newborn year,
candles still to be lit,
and nothing but starfish,
starfish on the beach.

Dinner With Her Ex

New-fangled fancy chilli-vinegar bottles,
I have to say in my defence,
my absolutely necessarily,
absolutely completely deliciously,
rat-arsed defence,
can – almost, in a certain seductive light, I swear –
be virtually visually indistinguishable from red wine.
But try telling that amid his histrionic spurting, gagging,
the frantic back-slapping, ruined tablecloth, her
'I'll deal with you later' glancing glares, and me
wondering when I'll be sufficiently sober to care.

This is a Controlled Poem

This is the benchmark, the vice of neutral,
the control experiment, the yardstick
by which others will be measured.
This is the voice of reason, that's reasonable, isn't it?
Hardly treason or inciting a revolution.
This is the sensible shoe – well heeled,
complimenting the weekend wax jacket of authority.
This poem is a Golden Labrador, The Sunday Times,
a bay-windowed Victorian semi,
a neatly pressed shirt for the office on Monday.
It won't let anyone into the traffic queue,
but it wouldn't cut anyone up either.
Middle-of-the-road suburban pin-striped grey,
black-and-white poems are for extremists, idealists, rebels,
and losers like me.

The Waiting Room

She looks right at me, through me,
in sunshine and in shade.
Thin, middle-aged,
dangerously dark behind sunglasses.

Expensive bracelet wristwatch, black designer dress,
dull gold writhes against her collarbone,
jet-black hair, hard face sets dead against me.

The other woman, blonde,
sharp-breasted, pearls,
high cutting cheek bones,
hair tight as a safe.

She raises black eyebrows,
a hint of caprice, hint of more,
hints at everything.

The Birth of a Nation

It wasn't a miracle,
most things are born out of poverty.
There's nothing miraculous about poverty –
except maybe surviving it.
Maybe this was a country.
Maybe it was on its knees.
Black cassocks and white handkerchiefs,
puddles of rain and pee in the confessional.

If it was '56
there might have been a TV
with a hundred chairs around it.
Nobody smoked – even though they could,
television was like a glamorous woman – you had to look.
People danced in the streets them days,
old women were carried like gods,
children looked to the skies and
old gunmen lived in the shadows.

I was lined up against a wall in '62,
five guns pointed at me,
and those that had no guns
pointed fingers.
They were too busy talking shite to pull the trigger.

Other children were offered up like sacrifices,
more had flowers in their hair,
and nobody trusted a stranger on the train
all newspapers and mirrors.
We had suitcases then, full of oranges,
fastened with buckles, belts, and string.
Some laughed at new-fangled tinned spaghetti
while others lay flat,
dead upon the slab. Was it '67?

The 70s saw office blocks and typewriters,
men in boiler suits running from the factory
smiling at going home, for good.
Others wore placards with words I could not see,
big boots and helmets surrounded them
while established suits whispered on the corners
and posters were torn down.
The big eye remained watching you in '72

Women started dressing differently
one waved a large red flag
I think there may have been tear gas,
mass rallies and raised fists,
some children screamed
though we laughed in school in '76

Was there an earthquake in 1980?
People carried children as rubble lined the streets,
this was a new era, I remember colour, not black and white,
models and weddings and sculpture, bright as stark colour

Bold and new the 90s,
night time was warm, petrol pumps were idle,
and trains stood still.
Shadows were now ghosts and tables overturned.
Life at the horse's gallop, beyond the boundaries,
art was on the walls, priests were flat on the floor,
things that didn't crumble were held by ropes and
poor Jesus was still on his cross.

The next gun was Lara Croft in 2002,
microphones and cleavage,
white dresses, scraped black hair and lipstick.
Even tunnels were full of light!
People kissed, paddled a canoe up the river,
a million cars waiting at the docks,
black men from Ghana cut each others hair and smiled,
we bathed in the sun.

One lay dead dripping blood crimson on white,
others raised fists behind the smoke,
but that was 2003.
It was like a football match and we had won,
Heineken, colour, Coca Cola,
and streetside cafés, lost paper dreams,
the birth of blind vision,
the discipline of design, faith
and the confessions of a
long-distance banker.

Time to park the Honda 50.

I am a Crooked Line

And I've walked a crooked mile,
sang every crooked song,
wished for sixpence,
though none the richer
with the Devil at the stile.
Life was brutal,
kittens never made cats,
rain barrel bound, drowned,
except the one that caught mice,
we let it stay, though
we let everything else go
in that crooked little house.

Spuds laughed on the plate,
sods of turf wafted sweet in the grate,
before the lorries of change like thunder
on the one way tarmac road.
Before Tony hung himself.
Before I was afraid.
Before the heavy rains.
Before the storms that raged
in every crooked line.

Profiterole Poets

Us and them, you and me,
and sometimes, always,
me.
Well 'X' used a gun,
I know his question well –
it was not the answer.
Still I'd like to say 'Fuck you' – 'fuck all of you!'
Happy-slappy back-clappy cunts
eating the gorgeous cake of yourselves.
I'd like to say a million things with nothing,
because nothing
is all I desire.

With Scant Regard for Wordsworth

I wandered lonely as a Cavan camel
that floats on high o'er dung and ghost estate,
when all at once I saw a crowd,
a host, of golden speculators ignoring
beside the lake, a naysayer among trees,
fluttering and pissing in the breeze.

Impoverished as the stars that shine
surviving on Mars Bars and Milky Way,
hands stretched in never-ending line
along the margin of the dole Q:
ten thousand saw I at a glance,
hanging their heads in deathly trance.

The speculators beside them danced;
threw mocking waves in glee:
a poet could not but be any less use,
in such impotent company:
I gazed – and gazed – but little thought
how us to our knees their wealth had brought:

For oft, when on my couch I lie
in pissed or in petulent mood,
they flash upon that inward eye
which is the bane of solitude;
and then my heart with hatred fills,
for their greed among the daffodils.

In the Zone

Bubbling in the bloodstream, SHINING!
Sell your soul for fifteen minutes on this street.
Buy yourself an Island just to name it 'No Man'.
Like all Stone Roses I want to be adored,
don't want to be bored,
there is a small paradise on the edge of every corner,
starfish on the pavement, jewels in our eyes,
like stars, like dreams, like a reality.
The very best of anything,
Fat Rat's lunatic sewer soup,
blood-stained crack pipes,
hope twitching at the end of a rope,
styrofoam chalice offered up from
twenty feet below the bottom rung,
look at us!! Boardwalk Jewels,
we shine! Oh! But how we shine!

In Flanders Fields by John McCrea with word associated inertia and the certainty of confusion

The loss of control
(poppies grow, do poppies still grow?)
And there was a gene, is there a gene?
twenty-four hours without a drink
would be a personal best –
Georgie Best, I spent a childhood in adoration.
In the aim of the father and the son and the holy spirit,
uisce beatha.

Would water by any other name taste as sweet?
And I supported Northern Ireland
because of him, a prize Plastic Paddy in Noddy Land
odd cod fish without blessed water.
And I wore his cheap plastic football boots,
so I could bleed for him.

(And then In Flanders fields the poppies blow
Between the crosses, row on row,
That mark our place; and in the sky
The larks, still bravely singing, fly
Scarce heard amid the guns below.)

The Messiah (a lifetime too late),
yards from me walking with Rodney Marsh,
his angel Gabriel,
and I left the van and I ran
while car horns and human glares
blared, I didn't care,
it was after the bomb
and I had lived though
still my ears rang with racist taunts.

I ran like I had run from school,
there he was in the flesh and rain,
my childhood unwound in every step,
reality tore at my lungs till within ten feet
this lifetime facade fell like scales
from my eyes.
I looked; and saw; and
turned away.
(To you from failing hands we throw
the torch; be yours to hold it high.
If ye break faith with us who die
We all die and this too shall pass
We shall not sleep, though poppies grow
will always grow in Flanders fields.)

Summer up at Oxford

River flat as day old champagne,
corridors and cloisters,
bleep and boosters,
Jeeves and Woosters,
brown brogues, corduroys,
bums in Beemers,
hooray for Henry,
victory for Victoria,
ties over shoulders
of the Bullingdon Boys.
Bicycles and biscuits
quadrangle tangles,
peppermints and spangles,
keep off the grass!
This is it, this is us,
welcome to our world!
Keep to ourselves
calm in a crisis,
what a carry on,
we put the ice in Isis,
we are your future,
we are your doom.

10 to the Power of 158

(close to a love poem)

Fine line architecture,
molecules of meltdown.
Two hearts left in the snow
could be identical,
but who would know?
They say, the odds of it happening
are indistinguishable from zero.
We say, fuck you!
I'll bury the burden,
I'll put the weight on you,
plunge bars and dimes,
stars and scars,
forever at the fair,
spinning wheels,
summer evening air,
two armed bandits,
time stands still as you blink,
every explanation,
kills the mystery.
Give me suspense
while I listen too intently,
not hearing at all.
I'm falling apart at these scenes.

The Streets of Our Town

Walk through the streets of Our Town
boarded-up shop fronts,
embrace the seaside colours of warm aerosol.
People don't piss for poetry in these streets,
heads filled with diesel fumes,
no breathing room for two to pass.
Dreams no longer burn,
hearts beat too long.
Walk through the streets of Our Town
time rolls back through the day
like dull eyes shine on crystal meth.
Souls sifted in time's cleansing flame.
Death wears a hoodie
on the streets of Our Town.

Don't ask William Blake.
Don't beg for mercy,
whatever you do,
just don't!

Dog Day Sunday

Rhythm yes, a
harmony of sorts,
a gospel choir of thoughts.
Life's breath, yes,
but laboured; shallowed; scarred.
I see, I hear,
full moons and jet planes,
darkness on the borders.

The Summer in Siam

Remember how the stars shone
for us alone, we stole each one,
lit up our dreams in coloured sleep?

Leave autumn's blind
indifference for times
stark trembling delirium,
russet leaf and fallen gold.

Let late winter's necessity
be the closed gates by the cross,
give us a final dance
for who we were –
not what we became.

This fucked up world shaped us,
took our vibrant colour dreams
for blacks bleak crackle, and
flittered us freely,
like dead leaves
of a forgotten past.

Spring may come to
the mind's eye hot in Casablanca,
black and white in memoriam,
but these closed eyes under
penny weights, see only colour,
dream only of you, and
the summer in Siam.

Bleeding Heart

The night the riots began
I felt old, out in the cold,
caught between the devil
and the detail of the revolution.
The codes were lost, the codes
were moral, a helping strong hand,
ethics balanced against anger, against
subversion, against anarchy.

Last night I heard the screaming,
I wanted to call the police,
loud voices shouting,
people were in need,
people were broken down,
people were lost,
people were bloodied.
I prayed for change, I prayed for justice,
I prayed for a law to protect the vulnerable,
to insulate the poor. Who will listen?
Who will answer my prayer?

Cardboard Kings

Blood red sovereign exchange
'remember that thou art dust'
and… the brightness above? Well,
the shadows weave doubt,
hope subjugated under a cadaverous sky.
I cannot remember my dreams
before hell showed the needle's escape,
alone, sleeping rough in the park,
keeping the blood line
(Lines! Do your lines!) alive.
Black night on double yellows,
blind-locked beat-alley poets,
damned one-way streets shady,
shabby, darkling tarmac.
Our days float blind two inches above cobbles,
life's sleeping partners trading on borrowed time.
'We are The Cardboard Kings!'
by night we sink cans of Dutch Gold,
watching Liffey Boardwalk lovers weave
Midsummer Night's darkest dream,
our eyes spaced-out flying saucers
as they tango in moonlit oblivion to
Mammon's crack-burning ire.
They, ignoring only lost souls
never know that we, each night
in cutting-edge purgatorial desire,
witness spaceships and vultures,
hope and damnation,
demons and angels,
circling their god's magnificent spire.

God Woman

They weren't fish from the sea,
any more than blue bears were
black silhouettes of herself.
God Woman, mother of all,
making progress reach for the skies.
Evolution, not revolution,
parity sparks trouble,
labels starlit dreams uncalled for.
We all have a monkey
on our backs, crystal clear,
like blue is black in light relief.
I love the city, I hate the reality,
rapid-fire irritation jarring.
We knew it was wrong,
alchemy, conjuring.
Sing, sing, sing,
dark dread in the night time:
hearts on fire spark
blazing light,
they break my heart,
like an egg, like a question
cracked into the heat.
We, who could do anything, choose
to do this, or this, or this?

I know the answer.
If it's a poem, it has a million
beginnings, a million chances;
I'm just dreading the end.

Identity Theft

M6
Hard shoulder
Broken down
Beaten up
Money stolen
Left for dead
Gravel grazed
Fly-over
Concrete
Blood red
Far from
Who I
Was.

The Fire Starter of Love

I don't know why there's no y in fire,
we've taken the ex out of sex,
put to bed the lie in liar.
So where is the point
of no return?

There's danger in dangerous,
no mouse in mice, yet
you sense the heath in Heathcliff,
the want in Cathy,
do you feel the need in me?
We were meant to be,
a match made in tinderbox,
you may be hot as hell,
but this heat is almost in heaven.

As god is my witness
and in the detail,
there's no flame
without the smoke
and no smoke,
without the fire, so
let's burn baby, burn!

Star Lovers

Kiss me quick, kill me slow,
'Goodbye', forever on our lips,
shooting up stars,
sky bound lateral lovers,
moon beam pearls of wisdom and wit.
Do you feel it?
We can see them!
We are ready,
put them in a box,
like chocolates,
ribbon-tied, tongue-twisted
pictures painted like arterial rainbows
in the crimson arc of neon smoke.
Subterranean, safe and sound.
We filled the void
with the smallness of ourselves,
our closed petals daisies
were eyelids kissed,
and I said 'I love you'
more than the average amount of times.

The Bones of You

For Collette

Close to flying,
three sheets windward,
topless, beachless,
singing in doorways
knowing we would fit inside.
Winter no threat,
summer everyday,
petrol to burn,
naked arms,
breezeless,
so good looking,
as beautiful as only
young people could be.
The time of our lives
ticking slow,
before we were sure,
167 miles apart.
I drove them moonlit,
just to say 'Hello.'

The Little Death

1000 miles per hour
and it's a moment,
your moment.
The moment of your life
when you think this will last
for ever.
The plate spinning smooth,
all the plates spinning.
The planets.
The satellites.
Perfect orbits,
sun up to sundown.
Those green eyes
as constant in an instant
as the North Star.
Chaos in abeyance,
the calm in the storm,
the centre of the whirlwind,
silence in the core.
Forever in the split second
on the brink of an eyelid that
closes like butterfly wings
on peace,
and opens to destruction.

The Loneliness of the Long Distance Drinker

They come and they go
from being there,
whilst you are never there,
always there.
They have homes to go to,
travelling with a sense of belonging,
the colours of the rainbow before them,
the light of hope above them.

God love them, saints preserve us.

I see the shadows one, two, then three.
I no longer fear them,
the shadows are me.

Water Dreams

Double yellow lines
110 miles per hour
Sal solo
Joe Stalin does what he says
On the tin
We're in deep
Water
H2O
Bottled up
Rapid flow
Flood plains
Stagnant jest
Safety vest
Hurricane west
East of Java
Key Largo
Orson Welles
Wells Fargo
Water waiter
Walter Matthau
H2O
Drip drip
In the night
Incandescense
Lack of sleep
Liquid dreams
Molten skies
Curly fries
Water water
I drink as much as I oughta
Free flowin lip smackin
Water? Yeuch!
Fish fuck in it.

Don't Stone Her

We all agree, that's terrible, barbaric.
She should be saved.
She should be shot.
She should be on death row.
A lethal injection.
Her crime was no crime.
And where is he?
He should be shot.
Look at their country,
it's all wrong, invade it,
Make it civilised like ours,
bomb the fuckers,
kill her, save her,
but not that way,
not in those colours,
not on that day, do it this way,
you don't want to do it like that,
this is how you do it,
that's the way to do it,
gottle-a-gear,
someone's stolen the sausages,
call the police, batter the crocodile,
batter the wife,
we're all civilized here,
all local people,
none of that round here!

Saturday Night Fever

Such a dull thud
bruising punch,
incongruous from
the vicious sharp edge.

What cruel years
could conspire our fates
so confined, conjoined?

Siamese switchblade,
a single flat second
this lively dark night.
Brother against
running loose,
lost in the ache
that leads fear to brave
the demons to drum
the beat of kill, or be,
kill, or be, kill and

fill the void,
colour the darkness
with stark life's blood bleeding red.

The Price of Love

Some women would kill a dragon for you,
some women put their tongue in your ear
so they can look across a crowded room.

Some men make mistakes,
some women carry them
for nine months,
or a lifetime.

The more I said 'I love you'
the nearer we drew
to the end.

Some men would kill for a pint,
life is cheap these days.

Rules of engagement (Subsection 3)

Never stand
When you can sit
Never sit when you can lie
Never lie when you can
Not give a fuck
Never swear when you can spit
Never spit when you can rage
Never rage when you can rail
Never rail when you can punch
Never punch
When you can stab
Never stab
When you can
Get a gun in your hand
Never run when you can lie
Never lie when you can fight
Never fight when you can lose
Never win if there's nothing to lose
Never war when you can bomb
Never plain bomb when you can nuke
Never nuke when you can
Hold the balance
In your sweaty little palm
A doll within a doll
Within us all

Best Days of Your life

School was a great education,
set me up for life,
showed me the blessed light
and lead me to the shadows.
School made me hollow,
taught me that I knew nothing,
that I was not correct,
that I was different,
that I could not learn,
that I did not belong.

School taught me that I was weak
and how to be afraid
sowed the seeds of doubt,

for factory/office/bar.
Still those fuckers have me
in the palms of their hands,
a kid on the inside looking out,
now on the outside looking in.

Or…

Education the blessed light the great salvation liberation
leveller moulder maker mover and shaker a kaleidoscoper a
rope of dark the hollow deep the seeds of doubt the
incorrect the weakness the fear to not belong sap confidence
self esteem identity entity essence branded they'll always
know you know nothing say nothing do nothing be nothing
a no-one a nobody just fill the gaps make way know your
place skirt the shadows don't get above your station escape
there is no escape from cradle to grave marked man target
practice schooldays continue to blight all your life. Watch.

What is it Good For?

I fought for you and
you fought for me, and
we fought (apparently)
for liberty.
I stuck a bullet
in another man's throat
to give him freedom of speech.

We blew a small boy to pieces,
they stitched him back together again,
all the Queen's surgeons
and all the President's men
told Humpty Dumpty to be grateful
that his mom and dad could vote,
if they were still alive.

What are they trying to do to me?
Give me a medal?
A heart attack?
A breakdown?
Told me it was the right thing to do,
then stick him back together again minus arms and legs
with glue.
Are they fucking with my mind?
Are they fucking with my life?
Are they fucking with the world?

Who is the real enemy?
Who holds the absolute power?
Absolute absolution,
Emperors in their new war clothes,
should we kill them, or
forgive them, though they know well what they do?
Maybe we should just say
NO, no more, fuck you!

Weekend

Fell flat faces frown
from silent fences,
shootings in the alley,
blood and bullets,
pricks of desire poison rush.
She needs only that I love her,
tap, tap, tap, ice sugared veins
crackle-creep, deep infused.
Worms turn black in the earth,
eyes blank, roll back in your head,
and world, my world, backwards turns
tonight like 10,000 lost days
spinning free.

(Brown trout jumping
forgotten streams sing
Windmills turning lazy slow tines
Trees sweetly blooming
Warm sun filtering through
Smiles of pure bred cotton white)

Slow and onwards
time travelling beneath the arches,
from the rooftops warm lit panes
beam skywards,
lamppost posters of lost faces,
ghosts from Christmas past.
The sky was the limit, now
damp brick black alleyway,
where six degrees of starlight
is five degrees
further than a man's
blackened heart can fall.

Cousins

What's the difference between nine and ninety behind bars
when your eyes burn back to
the point of no return?
I shot my flesh, my own blood,
on the bridge at Westport in the county Mayo
and never a word was spoke as the bullet flew
from victim to victor.
Though I survived while he thrived –
the Celtic tiger his master –
I with biro ink
bore love and hate
upon black bled knuckles.
Passions rise high in the vulnerable,
sang-froid belongs to the already dead,
I did my time, years, so sweet their pain,
bartered against eternity
and the loss of soul
the loss of faith,
the cheap shot,
the shallow grave,
hollow the victory
and still I bleed.

Introspection

I turn the eye inwards
See the deep dark of me
that all the oceans of the world
could not hope to fill.

Romantic Ireland Retched and Wrung

Dead and gone,
cold shouldered in The International
A drunken parody, a plastic Saint Francis,
broken and betrayed,
sandwiches soup and beds made
in namesake dungeon, 15 Merrion Row.
Kavanagh his ghost to be seen
in the obscene boredom and neglect
nurtured in McDaids off Grafton Boulevard

Left to the postcards, the bar flies,
who will remember to weep?
The vultures have their pick,
dole out the drugs 1-2-3.
Behan, battered nobody,
buried in some forgotten hole.
She lives on within us,
this muse, or
without us,
ferried off to some foreign land,
or dead,
like O'Leary in his grave.

Summer Long

I remember when dreams were dreams, not memories,
and we wore platform shoes,
and train tracks led to somewhere –
not the hell out!
I remember when the sun shone and reddened our necks,
when we pumped water from the well,
the cold clarity taking away our breath.
Our rough hands healed quicker than
our tender hearts.
Nothing was forever,
that was for the old, something we
would never be.
Fortunes came in a pack of cards,
chances on the dancefloor,
a different girl each week. Like the seasons
things bloomed then fell by the canal.
Walking to Gleeson's bar we knew that
the river was too wide, the winters were too wild,
so we sat in summer's buttercup meadows
making love while we could.

The Man Whose Head Exploded

Thinking.
That's a trip you don't want to take!
Stick to the familiar,
watch Eastenders, or
take up knife fighting.
Stay in the shallow end of life,
tie an umbilical cord to bring you back.
Thinking takes you out of your depth,

thought is a poetry death wish,
your mind's eye a microscope
poised above the Petri dish,
watching a million things divide and multiply.

Can you try this jacket on for size?
See how it wraps you tight,
saves you from yourself.
Think of it as a life jacket,
no strings attached.
Except of course that there ARE strings
attached –
Padded walls? Suits you sir!

So the thoughts collide and bounce and bark
like Pavlov's dog each time your alarm bell rings.
Whispers shout louder than things
that go bump in the night,
more fragile than you might think,
than you might…imagine.
And then the answers! Oh! The answers.
A billion bacteria for each amoeba.
That's when your head explodes.

Buckfast Breakfast

And I or he,
noises outside or inside the walls,
shuffled in shoes or bare feet,
sanding the lino.
Litter on the table,
sweep it to the floor.
Silence.

Freezing footsteps in the snow,
Christmas Eve,
the jewelled prize,
a black box.
Your brother shot someone
that slept with his wife.

Money makes the man and the machine, work.
Coins. Trap doors, pulleys, dumb waiters,
this is about poverty, this is about revolution,
this is the inside of your head.
Things roll like stones, crackle on the floor,
knives, forks, tools.
There's a queue for hell, civilised as you like,
(pause, action, rewind, stop, go).
Put the chain around your neck,
the instructions make no sense
with or without glasses.
Clay in their hands,
the thin line walked,
the floor is cold and dirty,
it's your turn, in you go,
the rats are waiting,
catch their tales,
tie them up in knots,
over and again.

Whatever

Label warning signs.
These peanuts may contain traces of peanut.
These poems may contain excesses of pretentious bullshit.
You have been warned.

The Beautiful South

Guddle-me-fuddle
we're all in a muddle,
whispering wound and a-blood-e-blood-e-blood.
And a say nothing, and a nothing is silence,
and no silence is golden,
and pieces of silver go clink-a-clink a clinkety-clink.
Then lick-a-lick a lickety-lick the wounds
clean as a whistle, blower blow-a-blow a-blowing.
What-oh-what are we showing,
a terrible racket this poetry business?

The Train to Aberystwyth

I had a ticket, a lift to the station
early morning from Uncle Liam, granite man.
The great escape, windows and fields flying by,
every passing house another few bricks away from home,
everything noosed me to the seat.

The train to Aberystwyth
left from Reading or Watford and changed at Crewe.
It was meant to try and save me,
a lifeline thrown, clickety-clack.
Beer and sandwiches, heaven on a plate,
stale dust from faded velvet
rising red in morning light.
Hearts can carry heavy weight,
'Clickety-clack, don't look back.'

Trains to Aberystwyth always leave,
they never arrive, lost in self,
reflections of faces in the window,
a thousand breaths of relief hypnotic,
'Don't look back, clickety-clack'
passing over gravel and sleepers,
iron wheels rhythmic, spark steel tracks.
'Always-there never-back'
'Always-there never-back'
Always there.

The City Wakes

Let myself breathe,
let the early morning mist rise,
no good corking it like a genie.
Magic is what you make of it.
I don't hear swirling Gershwin melodies,
I don't see what can't be heard,
I can't stop the pictures forming
on the inside.
Coffee will kiss sleep away,
a siren sings 'Rockferry'.
She's not that kind,
are any of us?

Sunglasses

Enigmatic chic for the masses,
men will make passes at girls
who wear sunglasses.
What mystery do we hide behind them?
Women and men, insect-eyed aliens
blocking out the sun, keeping in the mystique
winter and summer if you're the drummer
in a famous band, shivering at Sandycove,
or sizzling at St. Tropez.
Head to Dunnes in April or May, June or July,
whenever you fly to sunnier shores
where shades are worn indoors
(that's for the uber cool
not in Mullingar
in Murphy's lounge, you'd look a fool)
I want a giant pair with writing on
like Lennon,
(Jinx not John)
or mirrored and bright
to cover the bloodshot eyes
when I look a sight.
I'm buying them now while they are cheap
a half-price winter bargain that I can keep
till the Summer comes.

This Christmas We

Stretch the fabric of life,
buy kerosene by the gallon,
cut washing-up sponges in two,
surf supermarket car parks
for the abandoned trolley's
shiny reward.
We raid jam jars,
pluck forgotten coins from sofa, armchairs,
old coats, trousers, and dusty drawers.
We drink brought home Spanish Brandy
from other people's holidays,
we mend,
we contract,
cut-back,
shrink and save,
we winnow
but keep it all.
We are not yet old,
not yet finished
we reduce,
re-use, recycle.
We cope, we survive
in first world luxury,
rejoice in hope
and are glad.

Photograph: Collette O'Donoghue

PEADAR O'DONOGHUE has had poems published in *Poetry Ireland Review, The SHOp, Revival, Bare Hands Poetry, Can Can, The First Cut, Outburst, Census 3* and *The Burning Bush*. He has also published flash fiction in *Ink Sweat and Tears*. He founded, runs, and edits *The Poetry Bus Magazine*, an innovative journal of art, fiction and poetry, accompanied by a CD of the poets reading their work. An accomplished photographer, Peadar's photos have been selected for a solo exhibition at The Signal Art Gallery, Bray and group exhibitions for Wicklow Arts Office and The Mermaid Arts Centre, Bray. They have been published in *The Stinging Fly* journal (and anthology) and *The SHOp*, including the front covers. They have also been published in *Magma* and *The Dubliner*.